MTR 100439

MITRE TECHNICAL REPORT

MITRE

Multiple Encounter Dataset (Deceased Persons) MEDS-II

Data Description Document

Andrew P. Founds

Nick Orlans

Genevieve Whiddon

Version 4.0

December 22, 2010

NISTIR 7807

NIST Special Database 32
Multiple Encounter Dataset II (MEDS-II)

Data Description Document

Andrew P. Founds
Nick Orlans
Genevieve Whiddon
MITRE Corporation

Craig Watson
Information Technology Laboratory
Information Access Division

February 2011

U.S. Department of Commerce

National Institute of Standards and Technology
Patrick D. Gallagher, Deputy Director

Acknowledgement

This dataset is being released (as prepared by MITRE Corporation) to support the NIST Multiple-Biometric Evaluation 2010 (MBE). In addition, this dataset is available to any user interested in biometric research. The sponsor of this joint effort and provider of the data is the Federal Bureau of Investigation (FBI).

MTR100439

MITRE TECHNICAL REPORT

MITRE

Sponsor: FBI CJIS
Dept. No.: G123
Contract No.: J-FBI-07-164
Project No.: 1410FC09
Downgrade UNCLASSIFIED
Derived By:
Declassify On:

Multiple Encounter Dataset (Deceased Persons) MEDS-II

Data Description Document

Andrew P. Founds

Nick Orlans

Genevieve Whiddon

Version 4.0

December 22, 2010

Table of Contents

List of Figures

List of Tables

1 Overview

This document and associated dataset is an update to the Multiple Encounter Dataset I (MEDS-I), originally published by the National Institute of Standards and Technology (NIST) in May 2010[1]. The MEDS is a test corpus organized from an extract of submission files of deceased persons with prior multiple encounters. A submission file is an electronic file containing biographic and biometric data recorded during an encounter of an individual. The submission files conform to the specifications defined by the Electronic Biometric Transmission Specification (EBTS) extension to the American National Standards Institute (ANSI)/NIST Information Technology Laboratory (ITL)-1-2007 standard[2].

MEDS-I and MEDS-II are intended to stimulate research and to assist with the NIST Multiple Biometric Evaluation. The MEDS-II update approximately doubles the number of images, and extends the metadata to better support research and evaluation on pose conformance and local face features. These data are provided to assist the FBI and partner organizations refine tools, techniques, and procedures for face recognition as it supports Next Generation Identification (NGI), forensic comparison, training, analysis, and face image conformance and inter-agency exchange standards. The MITRE Corporation (MITRE) prepared MEDS-I and MEDS-II in the FBI Data Analysis Support Laboratory (DASL).

This paper describes the basic properties of the images and some relevant image quality characteristics that pertain to collection practices and the calibration and evaluation of face recognition technology. Table 1 provides an overview of the final contents of the MEDS-I and MEDS-II corpus.

Table 1 – MEDS-II Dataset Overview

Dataset	Subject Count	Submission Count	Image Count
MEDS-I	380	682	711
MEDS-II	138	535	598
MEDS-I & MEDS-II	518	1,217	1,309

All original submissions contain at least one logical Type-10 record, the record type within the ANSI/NIST-ITL 1-2007 file format reserved for face images and Scars, Marks, and Tattoos (SMT) images. The submission files were parsed into the various record types, as described below in Section 2.

---

[1] Watson, C. I. (2010, May 10). NIST Special Database 32 – Multiple Encounter Dataset I (MEDS-I). Retrieved December 13, 2010, from National Institutes of Standards and Technology: http://www.nist.gov/itl/iad/ig/sd32.cfm

[2] American National Standard for Information Systems – Data Format for the Interchange of Fingerprint, Facial, and other Biometric Information – Part 1. NIST Special Publication 500-271, May, 2007. Online: http://fingerprint.nist.gov/standard/Approved-Std-20070427.pdf

2 Data Preparation Methodology

This section describes the processes of EBTS decomposition, data normalization and correction, and face detection necessary to prepare this corpus.

2.1 EBTS Data Decomposition

The submission files were parsed and examined using a combination of government, commercial, and custom EBTS parsing and reporting tools to help verify consistent results. Table 2 presents a summary of tools used.

Table 2 – Tools used to parse and examine submission files

Tool	License	Developer	Purpose
Universal Latent Workstation	GOTS	Noblis[3]	Manual EBTS inspection
EFTSExtract	GOTS	MITRE	Batch extraction and reporting
Google Picasa	COTS	Google	Gallery viewing
PittPatt[4]	COTS	Pittsburgh Pattern Recognition	Tools for face detection
Stasm	N/A	S. Milborrow, F. Nicolls[5]	Annotation of face contours and features
MarkIt	GOTS	MITRE[6]	Face annotation and point editing
matplotlib	PSF	J. Hunter[7]	Data visualization

Each submission file contained an associated subject identifier to indicate the link between a subject and their encounters (i.e., submission files or recording events) over time. For many subjects in the set, more than one submission file was provided. Multiple encounters of individuals are sometimes referred to as *recidivist* encounters. The time interval between multiple encounters varies per individual. The cardinal relationship between subjects and submissions and samples is shown in Figure 1.

---

[3] http://www.noblis.org

[4] http://pittpatt.com

[5] Milborrow, S., & Nicolls, F. (2008). Locating Facial Features with an Extended Active Shape Model. *ECCV*, http://www.milbo.users.sonic.net/stasm.

[6] Pruitt, M. (1, June 2010). MarkIt. McLean, VA, USA

[7] Hunter, J. (2010, November 9). *matplotlib Release 1.0.0*. Retrieved December 13, 2010, from matplotlib: http://matplotlib.sourceforge.net/index.html

Figure 1 – Relationship between Subjects, Submissions and Biometric Samples

After establishing ground truth for this dataset (described in Section 3), the Type-10 images were assessed for their face content. Table 3 summarizes the image content as observed in the original submission files. Not all images are face images or considered part of the MEDS-II dataset.

Table 3 – Number of Type-10 Images and Submissions

Number of Images	Number of Submissions	Comments
1	1,217	1st image is frontal or near frontal face image
2	72	2nd image is usually a profile face image
3	20	3rd image is usually a profile face image

2.2 Data Normalization and Correction

The consistency and reliability of the biographic data in the submissions varies, presumably due to input error or inconsistent information collection from subjects who may not have cooperated with the process. Some data normalization and corrections were performed to alleviate these errors on the metadata relevant to face detection and recognition (e.g., dates, gender, and race fields).

The date of arrest (DOA) and photo date (PHD) should be, by definition, within close date proximity of each other, and the PHD should always follow the DOA if the dates are not identical. In instances where either of these dates was missing or corrupt, the most repeated date among the entries was used for analysis. In the accompanying metadata file, an indicator is used to identify which records had been modified from their original contents.

2.3 Face Detection and Pose Labeling

Executing automated face detection was the first step in distinguishing the face-containing images from non-face-containing images. The face-containing images were additionally delineated into frontal and non-frontal bins based on the PittPatt (the tool used for face detection) pose estimates. Human reviewers manually reviewed each category to remove residual errors and obtain the final ground truth for the subject's pose.

As shown in Table 4, below, 1,219 of the images are frontal or "near frontal", as determined by human review. Frontal images are defined as within 15 degrees horizontal of full frontal, as estimated by visual inspection. Near frontal is defined as within 45 degrees horizontal, but not overlapping with the defined yaw angle range for frontal. Profiles or "near profiles" are likewise within 45 degrees of full profile, although "two-eyed" near profiles may be closer to 45-60 degrees off full profile. These definitions are working definitions and are prone to human error. Images where the pose yaw angle is compounded with pitch and roll deviations are even more prone to human review variations.

Table 4 – Image Types

Type	Count	Comments
Frontal	858	$\approx [-15,15]$ degrees yaw angle
Near Frontal	361	$\approx [-45,-15) \cup (15,45]$ degrees yaw angle
Near Profile	6	$\approx (-60,-45] \cup (45,60]$ degrees yaw angle
Profile	85	$\approx [-90,-60] \cup [60,90]$ degrees yaw angle
Total:	1,309	

2.4 Recidivists and Match Pairs

Near profile and profile images are included in the dataset to benefit research and development; however, these images are omitted in the count of match pairs. After profile and near profile images were removed, the number of match pairs is based on the remaining frontal or near frontal images (1,219 images). Table 5 enumerates the number of match pairs over the subjects based on the number of images per subject. The table only refers to frontal and near-frontal images.

Table 5 – Enumeration of Match Pairs

Number of Subjects	Number of Images	Number of Match Pairs
262	1	N/A
124	2	124
47	3	141
22	4	132
15	5	150
12	6	180
9	7	189
9	8	252
4	9	144
6	10	270
5	11	275
1	13	78
1	16	120
1	18	153
	Total:	2,208

3 Description of Corpus

This section provides a summary of the subject metadata contained within the MEDS-II dataset.

3.1 Race and Gender

Race and gender information are based on observation or provided by the subject. Race can be ambiguous and ultimately is a social or cultural interpretation (as opposed to a consistently defined attribute for labeling). Race and gender, as provided in the data, is shown in Figure 2.

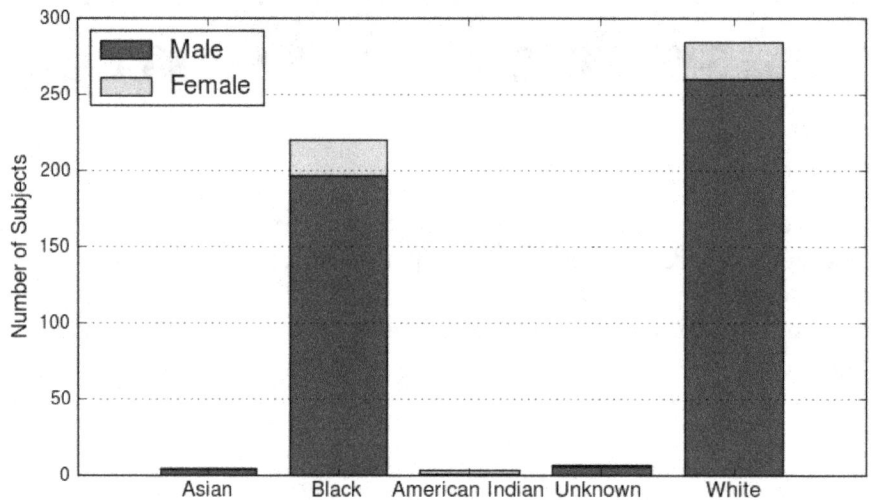

Figure 2 – Distribution of Gender by Race

3.2 Age Summary and Time between Encounters

Figure 3, below, illustrates the ages of the 518 subjects at the time the images were captured. The age of the subjects at the time of collection is also provided in the accompanying metadata for this dataset.

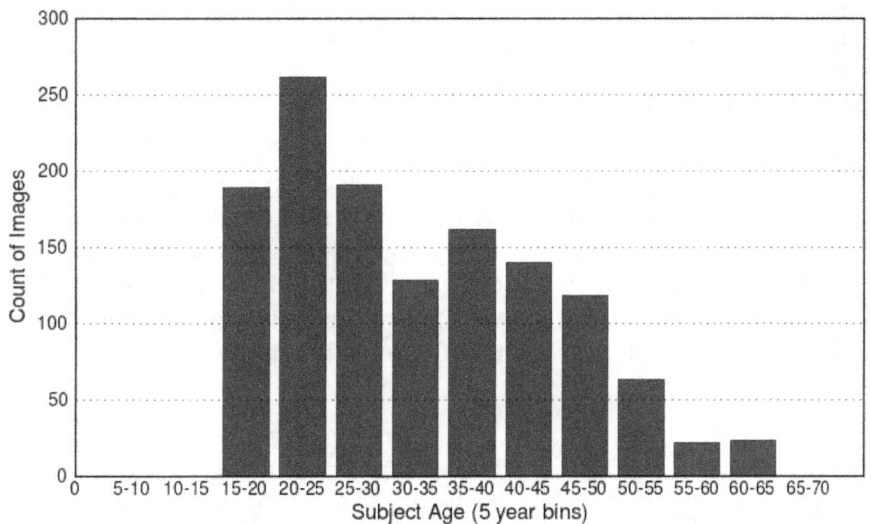

Figure 3 – Histogram of Subject Ages at Photo Date

Of the images in the dataset, 48% are of subjects between the ages of 15 and 30 years of age. Nine percent of the images in the dataset are of subjects greater than 50 years old while the oldest subject in the dataset is 69 years of age.

Figure 4 illustrates the times between the first and last encounter for all the subjects with multiple encounters. The horizontal axis is organized in bins of six month intervals.

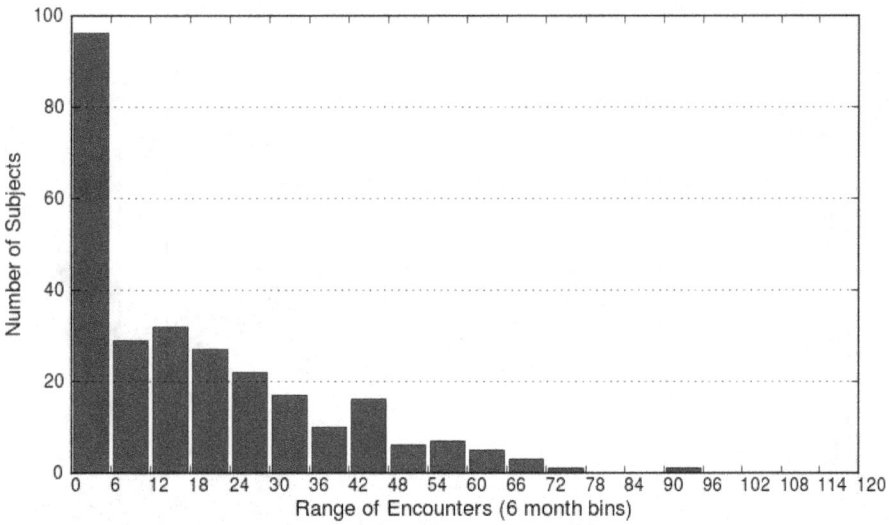

Figure 4 – Times between Encounters (e.g., first and last)

Of the times between encounters, 47% are less than one year. The remainders are between one and five years (49%) and greater than five years (4%).

3.3 Image Dimensions

Image sizes and approximate resolution of the face vary due to the use of different camera equipment and composition inconsistencies of the subject in the image frame. Figure 5 is comprised of three charts, a histogram which illustrates the number of images by width, a histogram which illustrates the number of images by height, and a scatter plot which illustrates the number of images by both height and width. Of the images' dimensions, 70% are approximately 0.3 megapixels while one image exceeds five megapixels. The red box in Figure 5 identifies the dimensions of roughly 70% of all images in the corpus.

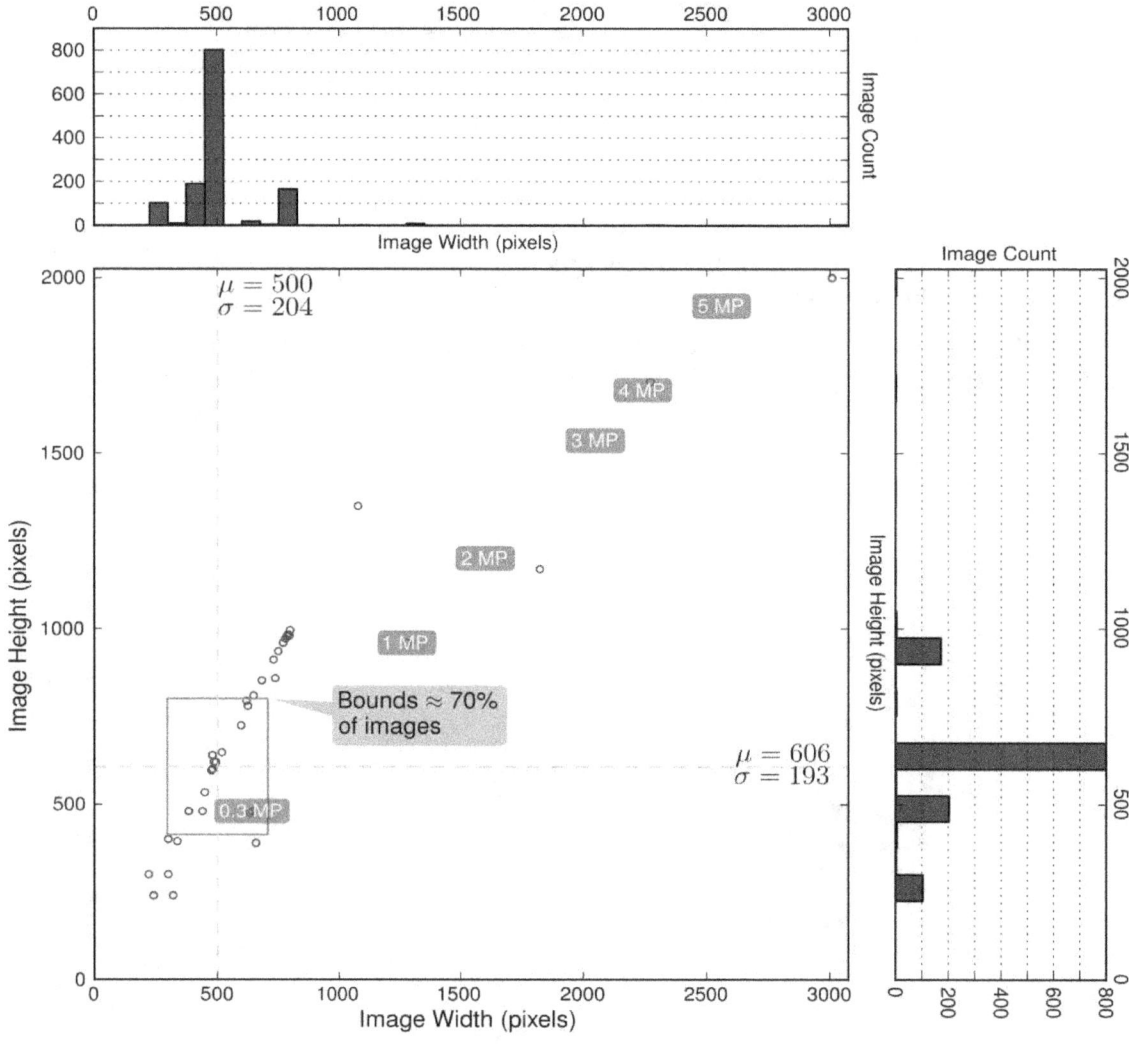

Figure 5 – Image Dimensions

According to section 6 of the current specification, the ITL has no image scanning resolution for Type-10 records: *"Facial/mugshot, SMT, and iris images rely on the total number of pixels scanned and transmitted and are not dependent on the specific scanning resolution used."*

3.4 Face Resolution and Subject Pose

Consistent face resolution requires consistent sizing and framing. The framing of the subjects in the MEDS-I and MEDS-II images varies and, in some instances, the full face is not visible. For the frontal and near frontal images, MITRE estimated interocular distances based on the outputs from automated face detection. The results presented in Figure 6 and Figure 7 are based on 1,219 images that have been identified as frontal or near frontal and are based on automated outputs that were not reviewed or adjusted by human review.

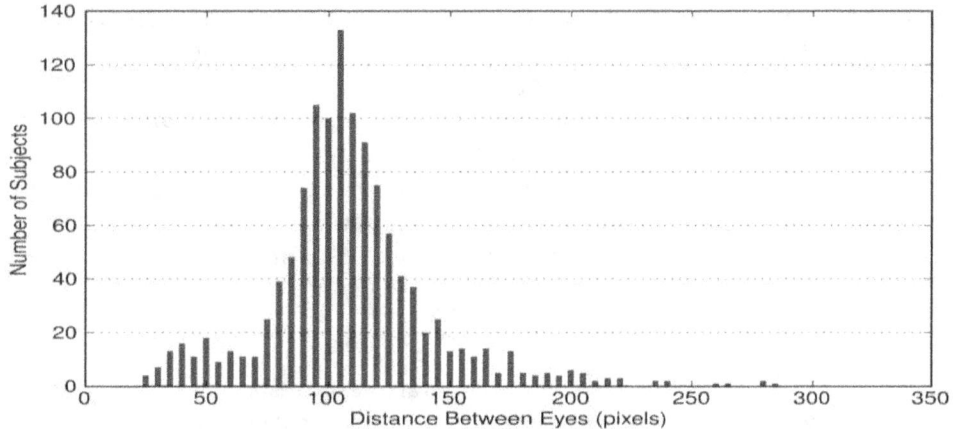

Figure 6 – Distribution of Estimated Interocular Distances (in pixels)

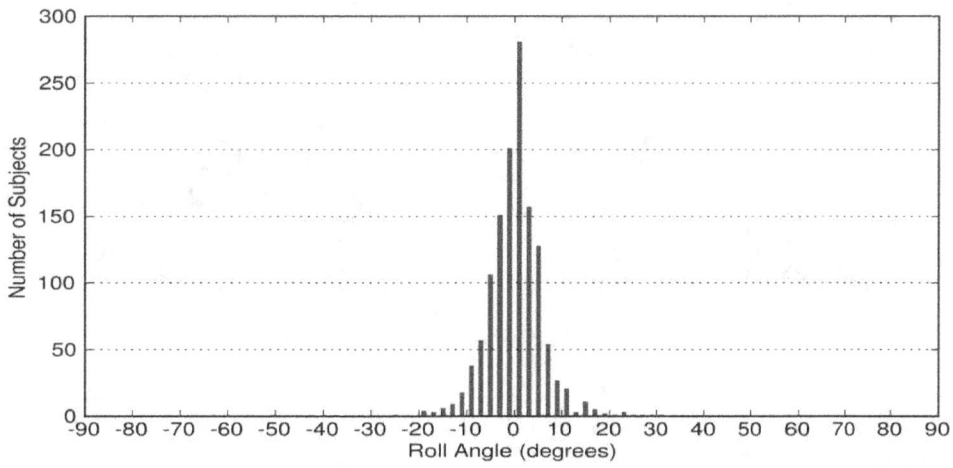

Figure 7 – Face Roll Angle (degrees from horizontal)

11

4 Face Landmarking

4.1 Landmarking Process

Accurate landmarking of face images indicates successful localization of facial features and also may help with determining pose estimation and conformance. The MEDS-II images include a set of facial landmarks output by Stasm, an automated face landmarking tool based on Active Shape Models (ASM). Stasm is designed to work on passport-style photographs or on frontal views with neutral expressions.

Although all MEDS-II images were processed using Stasm, a portion of the images required manual correction in cases where the Stasm points were deemed inaccurate. As with most computer vision techniques, Stasm's ability to locate face landmarks is not as accurate as a human, and will occasionally make errors. In certain circumstances, manual editing of Stasm points was done with a custom tool, MarkIt, developed for face landmarking. Based on MITRE's empirical evidence, those images that exemplify poor lighting or extreme subject expressions tend to contain numerous errors. Cropped images will have unusable or stray points. Among images that had to be annotated manually, the contour of the jaw line proved to be a predominantly difficult area for Stasm, particularly if the subject had a beard or the contour of the jaw line was of low contrast. Some low contrast images were observed to improve performance after the contrast was boosted; however additional analysis is required. Figure 8 shows examples of images with output Stasm points overlaid on the image.

Example of *Good* Stasm *Output Requiring No Manual Editing*

Example of Stasm *Output Requiring Manual Editing*

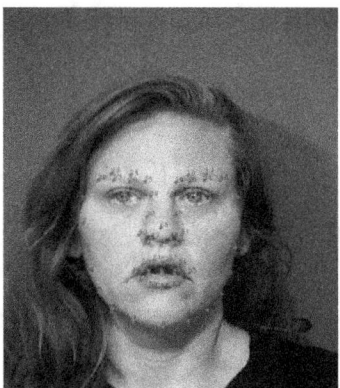
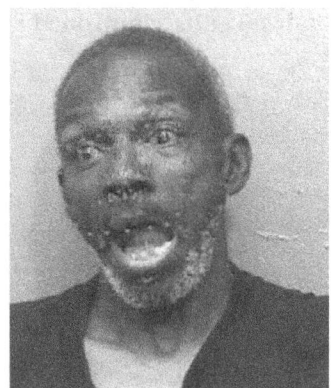

Figure 8 – Example Stasm Outputs

Stasm outputs a total of 68 points which correspond to an (x, y) pixel value in the image. Each point corresponds to a unique facial landmark. These points are depicted in Figure 9 and enumerated in Table 6.

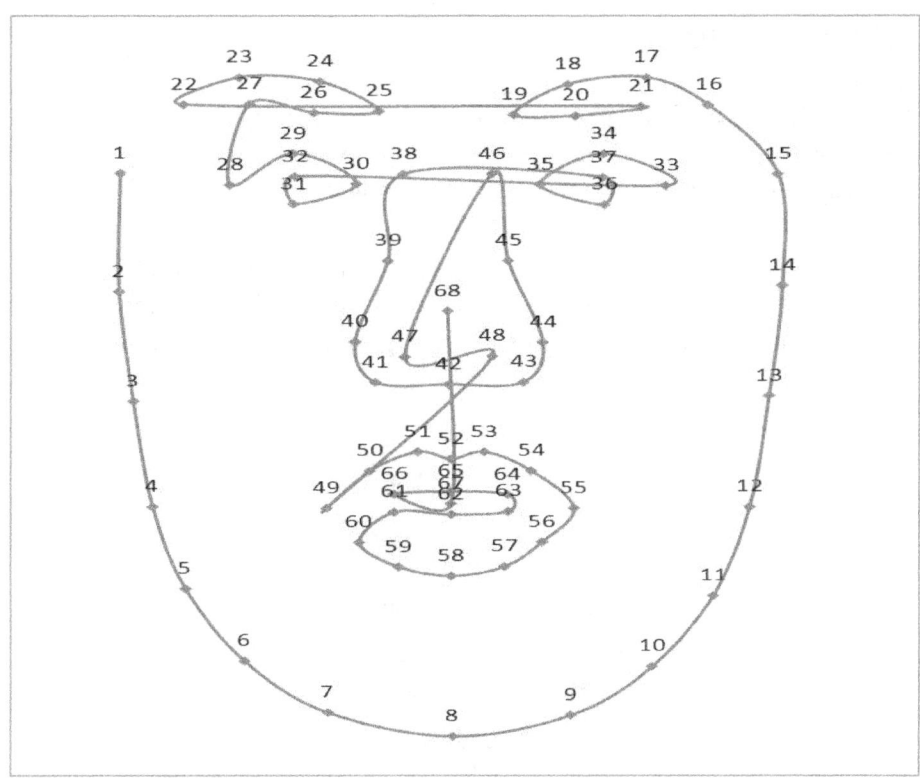

Figure 9 - Depiction of 68 Stasm Points

Table 6 - Listing of 68 Stasm Points

1. Right Temple	18. Left Eyebrow Inner Top	35. Left Eye Inner	52. Lip Top
2. Right Zygion	19. Left Eyebrow Inner	36. Left Eye Bottom	53. Left Lip Inner Top
3. Right Cheek Top	20. Left Eyebrow Inner Bottom	37. Left Pupil	54. Left Lip Outer Top
4. Right Cheek Bottom	21. Left Eyebrow Outer Bottom	38. Right Nasion	55. Left Chelion
5. Right Gonion	22. Right Eyebrow Outer	39. Right Alare Crease	56. Left Lip Outer Bottom
6. Right Chin Top	23. Right Eyebrow Outer Top	40. Right Alare	57. Left Lip Inner Bottom
7. Right Chin Bottom	24. Right Eyebrow Inner Top	41. Right Nostril	58. Lip Bottom
8. Menton	25. Right Eyebrow Inner	42. Subnasale	59. Right Lip Inner Bottom
9. Left Chin Bottom	26. Right Eyebrow Inner Bottom	43. Left Nostril	60. Right Lip Outer Bottom
10. Left Chin Top	27. Right Eyebrow Outer Bottom	44. Left Alare	61. Right Lip Bottom Center
11. Left Gonion	28. Right Eye Outer	45. Left Alare Crease	62. Bottom Stomion
12. Left Cheek Bottom	29. Right Eye Top	46. Left Nasion	63. Left Lip Bottom Center
13. Left Cheek Top	30. Right Eye Inner	47. Right Nose Tip	64. Left Lip Top Center
14. Left Zygion	31. Right Eye Bottom	48. Left Nose Tip	65. Top Stomion
15. Left Temple	32. Right Pupil	49. Right Chelion	66. Right Lip Top Center
16. Left Eyebrow Outer	33. Left Eye Outer	50. Right Lip Outer Top	67. Stomion
17. Left Eyebrow Outer Top	34. Left Eye Top	51. Right Lip Inner Top	68. Pronasale

4.2 Landmarking Results

Ninety-two percent (1,226 images) of the MEDS corpus was processed using the Stasm tool. In cases where the image was determined to be a profile, fingerprint, or marking (e.g., scar or tattoo), Stasm was not used and no landmark locations were generated. All Stasm result points were normalized according to the width and height of the image in pixels and subsequently compiled for analysis.

Nearly eighty percent of the images processed by the Stasm tool were considered acceptable by human analysis. In some cases, output could not be produced due to the tool's inability to detect a face. A summary of the percentage of images able to be processed by Stasm is shown in Figure 10.

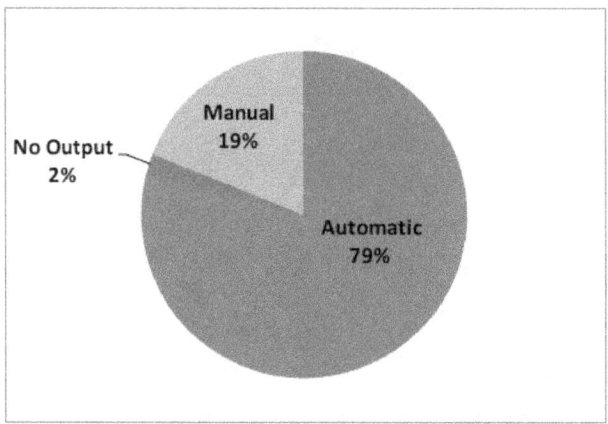

Figure 10 - Proportion of Automated vs. Manual Landmarking

Figure 11 and Figure 12 further isolate Stasm's ability to produce automated landmarks based on race and gender, respectively. MITRE postulates that the reason for performing a higher percentage of manual landmarking on Black or African American subjects is due to the lack of contrast between chin and neck in the image. Additionally, MITRE hypothesizes that male images having beards failed automated landmarking.

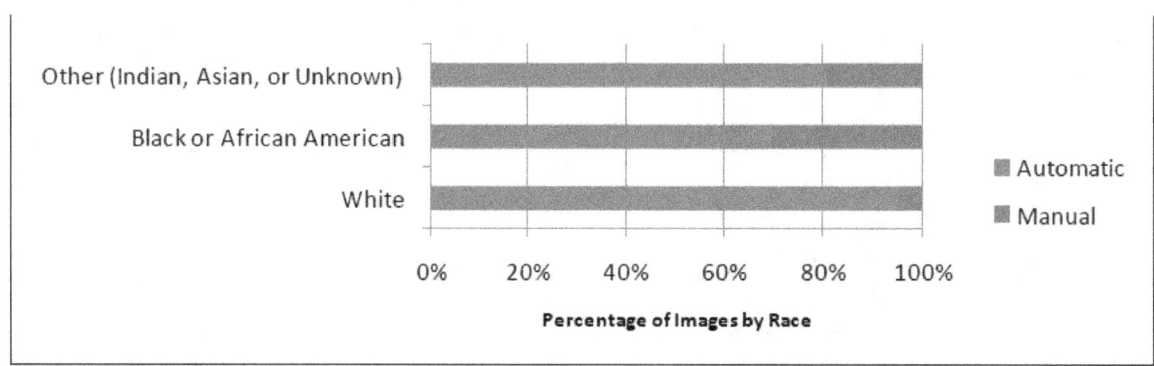

Figure 11 – Ability to Automatically Landmark Based on Race

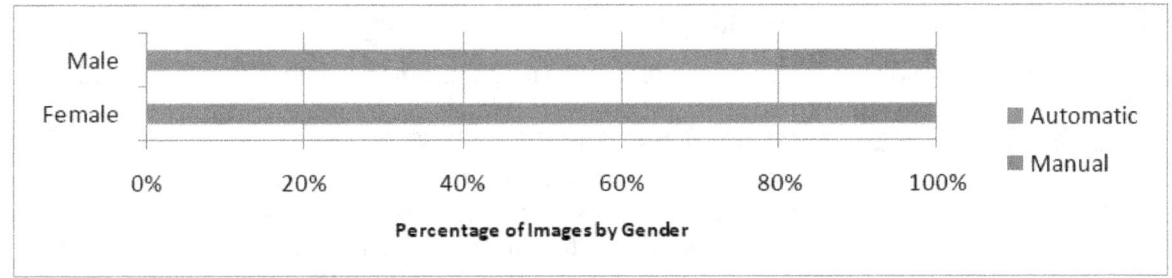

Figure 12 - Ability to Automatically Landmark by Gender

A high level analysis between PittPatt's confidence scores and yaw values, as correlated with Stasm output (e.g., rejection or acceptance by a human reviewer) was completed. Figure 13 and Figure 14 depict the correlation of confidence scores and yaw values, respectively, against Stasm's ability to successfully landmark an image. The impact appears to be minimal with little correlation between a confidence scores and yaw values.

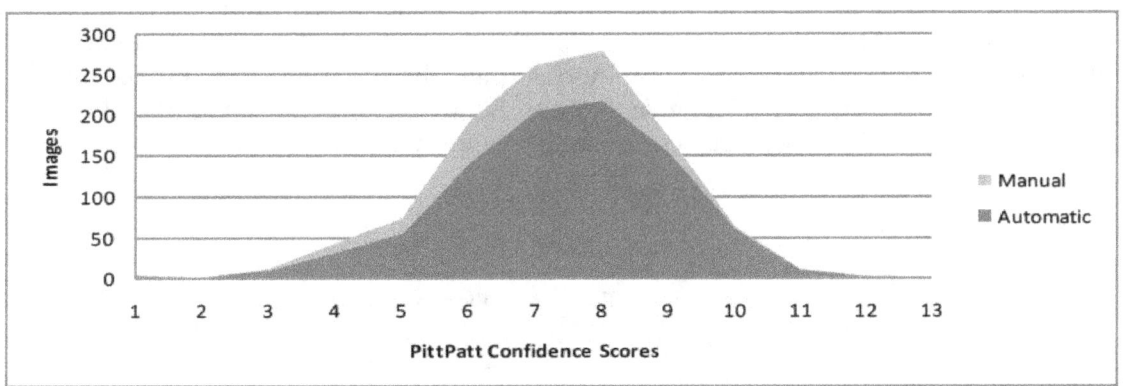

Figure 13 – Correlation of PittPatt Confidence Scores with Automated Landmarking

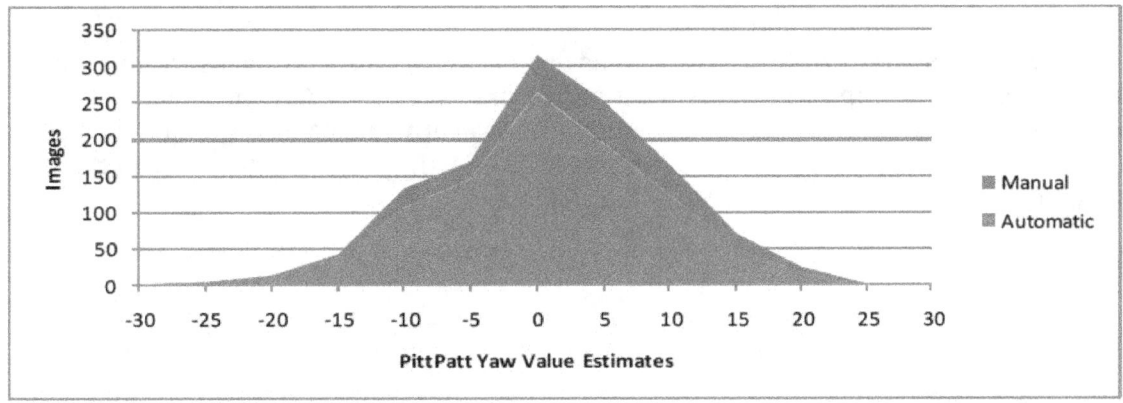

Figure 14 – Correlation of PittPatt Yaw Estimate with Automated Landmarking

4.3   Next Steps for Landmarking and the MEDS-II Corpus

The performance and robustness of facial feature localization is relevant to advancing face recognition and pose conformance, and there are certainly technology advancements yet to be achieved in this area. Additional analysis into the Stasm failures and comparative analysis with other landmarking approaches could be beneficial to recognition systems. Also of interest is to strengthen and better understand the relationships between face morphology (human observable features) and features utilized by machine recognition (i.e., Do they correspond in known ways or are they entirely divergent?).

5   Face Recognition and Imposters

Performance of face recognizers depends heavily on the fine tuning of two parameters: the false alarm rate and true acceptance rate. Imposters (i.e. non-mated subjects) are subjects identified in face recognition that are not true subjects, whose match confidence values are larger than the false alarm rate. MITRE performed a study of imposters to identify "look-a-likes" to highlight potentially problematic images for face recognizers.

As in the face detection study, MITRE has also used PittPatt to perform face recognition on the images which correspond to the 518 subjects in the corpus. As part of MITRE's experiment, the matcher threshold was set to 0.001% false acceptance rate to reduce the number of matched subjects in the results. Interestingly, there was a strong correlation between six non-mated subjects. Table 7 tabulates the number of hits on non-mated subjects and displays the images that correspond to imposters.

Table 7 – False Hits

Query Subject	Target Subject	Number of Hits
0388	0404	5
0471	0396	3
0471	0413	4

In Table 8 one can identify a few observations that generally cause problems within face recognition. First, all imposters in the set are comprised of African-American males, even though all subjects in the set were matched against each other. Second, the areas around the orbital region on the face appear to be similar to the human eye. Third, the shape of the nose of all imposters appears to be the same shape.

Table 8 – Results of Queried Images

Query Image	Result Images		
SUBJ-0388-08-01-14.jpg	SUBJ-0404-05-01-13.jpg	SUBJ-0404-04-01-11.jpg	
SUBJ-0388-16-01-01.jpg	SUBJ-0404-03-01-10.jpg	SUBJ-0404-05-01-13.jpg	
SUBJ-0404-05-01-13.jpg	SUBJ-0388-04-01-07.jpg	SUBJ-0388-08-01-14.jpg	SUBJ-0388-16-01-01.jpg
SUBJ-0471-01-01-05.jpg	SUBJ-0396-08-01-11.jpg	SUBJ-0413-06-01-03.jpg	

Results of Queried Images Continued

Query Image	Result Images		
 SUBJ-0471-03-01-01.jpg	 SUBJ-0396-04-01-03.jpg	 SUBJ-0396-07-01-05.jpg	 SUBJ-0413-01-01-08.jpg
	 SUBJ-0413-02-01-09.jpg	 SUBJ-0413-03-01-10.jpg	

Appendix A - List of Acronyms

Acronym	Expansion
ANSI	American National Standards Institute
ASM	Active Shape Models
BCOE	Biometric Center of Excellence
CW	Clockwise
CCW	Counter-clockwise
COTS	Commercial off the Shelf
DOA	Date of Arrest
DASL	Data Analysis Support Laboratory
EBTS	Electronic Biometric Transmission Specification
GOTS	Government off the Shelf
ITL	Information Technology Laboratory
MEDS	Multiple Encounter Dataset
MITRE	The MITRE Corporation
NCIC	National Crime Information Center
NGI	Next Generation Identification
NIST	National Institute of Standards and Technology
PHD	Photo Date
PSF	Python Software Foundation
SMT	Scars, Marks & Tattoos